Parrotfish

by Lola M. Schaefer

Consulting Editor: Gail Saunders-Smith, Ph.D.

Consultant: Jody Byrum, Science Writer,
SeaWorld Education Department

Pebble Books

an imprint of Capstone Press
Mankato, Minnesota

Pebble Books are published by Capstone Press
1710 Roe Crest Drive, North Mankato, Minnesota 56003
www.capstonepub.com

Library of Congress Cataloging-in-Publication Data
Schaefer, Lola M., 1950–
    Parrotfish / by Lola M. Schaefer.
    p. cm.—(Ocean life)
    Includes bibliographical references (p. 23) and index.
    Summary: Simple text and photographs introduce the physical characteristics
and behavior of parrotfish.
    ISBN-13: 978-0-7368-0247-5 (hardcover)
    ISBN-10: 0-7368-0247-9 (hardcover)
    ISBN-13: 978-0-7368-8218-7 (softcover pbk.)
    ISBN-10: 0-7368-8218-9 (softcover pbk.)
    1. Parrotfishes—Juvenile literature. [1. Parrotfishes.] I. Title. II. Series: Schaefer,
Lola M. 1950– Ocean life.
QL638.S3S335   1999
597'.7—dc21   98-31468

Note to Parents and Teachers

The Ocean Life series supports national science standards for units
on the diversity and unity of life. The series shows that animals
have features that help them live in different environments. This
book describes and illustrates parrotfish and their behavior. The
photographs support early readers in understanding the text. The
repetition of words and phrases helps early readers learn new
words. This book also introduces early readers to subject-specific
vocabulary words, which are defined in the Words to Know section.
Early readers may need assistance to read some words and to use
the Table of Contents, Words to Know, Read More, Internet Sites,
and Index/Word List sections of the book.

Printed in the United States of America in North Mankato, Minnesota.
042015   008873R

Table of Contents

4

Parrotfish are colorful.

Parrotfish live near coral reefs.

Parrotfish have
joined teeth.

Parrotfish teeth look like a beak.

algae

Parrotfish eat algae.

Some algae live
inside coral.

Parrotfish bite off pieces of coral to find algae.

Parrotfish eat the coral and turn it into sand.

Some beaches have sand made by parrotfish.

Words to Know

algae—small plants without roots or stems that grow in water; parrotfish eat algae.

colorful—having many colors; parrotfish can be blue, green, yellow, orange, purple, red, black, and white.

coral—an ocean animal with a soft body and many tentacles; parrotfish eat algae that grow inside the hard outer shells of corals.

coral reef—an area of coral skeletons and rocks near the surface of the ocean

sand—tiny grains of rock that make up the ocean floor, beaches, and deserts; parrotfish eat coral and make sand; a parrotfish can make up to five tons (4.5 metric tons) of sand each year.

teeth—bony parts of a mouth used for biting and chewing; parrotfish teeth are joined together and look like a bird's beak.

Read More

Cerullo, Mary M. *Coral Reef: A City That Never Sleeps.* New York: Cobblehill Books, 1996.

Pringle, Laurence P. *Coral Reefs: Earth's Undersea Treasures.* New York: Simon and Schuster Books for Young Readers, 1995.

Souza, D. M. *Fish That Play Tricks.* Creatures All Around Us. Minneapolis: Carolrhoda Books, 1998.

Internet Sites

FactHound offers a safe, fun way to find Internet sites related to this book. All of the sites on FactHound have been researched by our staff.

Here's all you do:

Visit *www.facthound.com*

FactHound will fetch the best sites for you!

Index/Word List

Word Count: 51
Early-Intervention Level: 12

Editorial Credits
Martha E. Hillman, editor; Steve Christensen, cover designer and illustrator; Kimberly Danger and Sheri Gosewisch, photo researchers

Photo Credits
Jay Ireland and Geogienne E. Bradley, 1, 8, 18
Photo Network/Hal Beral, cover, 4, 10
Rainbow/Dean Hulse, 16
Tim Wakefield and Steve Kempf, Department of Zoology and Wildlife Sciences, Auburn University, Ala., 12 (inset)
Tom Stack and Associates/Dave B. Fleetham, 12; Brian Parker, 14
Unicorn Stock Photos/John Schakel, Jr., 6; Florent Flipper, 20